Steam Memories on Shed: 1950's – 1960

No. 25: Southern Region En

T Butcher

ISBN 978-1-907094-72-9

INTRODUCTION

Having gone through the stage of a Hornby Dublo model railway, I became interested in railways again, but this time in the 'real thing' in 1955, at the age of 17. Starting with a very basic camera with only a 1/75th shutter speed, I got few even passable photographs. I then progressed to a relatively cheap 2¼ x 3¼ Kodak camera, which I bought with money from delivering parcels at Christmas for the Post Office in 1956. This at least had a 1/200th second shutter, and I did start to take some reasonable pictures in 1956.

During the late 1950s and early 60s' I went round most of the Southern Region engine sheds, although, as a student, I had no car or motorbike, so this was all by public transport - largely on the trains. I did obtain official shed permits for most of the sheds from Waterloo Head Office, and had to fit the dates to my holidays, etc., depending on where they were located. There were a few sheds I never got round in this period, such as Norwood Junction, for which even permits would not be granted, due I suspect to being situated in a fork of main electrified lines (although I actually think Guildford shed was more dangerous). I missed out on Yeovil Junction, and Faversham, and not until later in the 60's did I visit Weymouth, Templecombe (a very small shed) and Bath Green Park (the latter two serving the Somerset & Dorset Joint line), as well as one or two others.

Having lived in the south-east all my life until then, I naturally became first and foremost a 'Southern Man' with my railway interest and photography. Although the Southern Region had the smallest number of steam locomotives by a long way, it still possessed in this period a surprising number of interesting classes, including many of very old vintage. The M7 and E4 tanks (both introduced in 1897), as well as the H tanks (used on the Central & SE sections of the Region), particularly come to mind .There were still considerable numbers of these operating in the latter half of the 1950s (e.g. 61 E4s, 57 Hs and 103 M7s in the summer of 1956). There were also several classes of 4-4-0s surviving, including classes D (only to 1956), D1, L, L1, E1 and T9; all very good looking engines. Many old classes of tank engines still survived initially from 1956 onwards in small numbers, such as E1, R1, B4, G6, 0395 (Adams 1874) as well as the well loved A1/A1X, originally of 1872 vintage! This is not to mention small classes of older main line engines still in use like the beautiful Brighton Atlantics, the last three Drummond D15 4-6-0s, and the last of the 'Rememberence' class (designated NI5X). There were of course also very small classes of iconic engines still operating, in particular the Adams 4-4-2 tanks and the Beattie Well tanks. I guess that the longer survival of so many old engines was partly due to having been retained during the Second World War, and its austerity aftermath, and also because the Southern had a large amount of the region already electrified in the 1930s. The latter meant that the Southern did not need such a large fleet of main line engines as the other regions, although Bullied Pacifics and Maunsell 'Lord Nelsons' and 'King Arthurs' were still very much in evidence. The elimination of steam in the South Eastern Section in June 1961 – due to further electrification to the Kent Coast line – did of course hasten the end of many of these interesting old classes.

In this limited review of my SR shed photographs I hope you find something of interest, and of course quite a few survivors of these classes still survive in preserved form in museums, and even more excitingly some are running fully restored in working order on our many preserved railway lines.

Tony Butcher, Crawley Down, January 2013

Cover picture: **It is often forgotten just how dirty steam locomotives are/were. It was not just the locomotives either; their surroundings, be it an engine shed, workshop, station platform! They were all grotty to some degree, others obviously more so. The soot laden pathways in engine sheds for instance; never cleaned, the layers just kept building up, helped no doubt by tiny droplets of lubricating oils. This view at Nine Elms engine shed on 1st April 1958 allows the eye to take in detail which might otherwise have been ignored (modellers take note, although you are probably already spotting the various shades of grey, which would not be much different in colour). We are standing in an area which was known as the 'Old shed' before it was cut back in length after bombing damage in WW2. Ahead is a doorway into what was known as the 'New shed' with its ten roads covered by transverse pitched roofs which are nicely defined. The 'Old shed' consisted fifteen roads and we are looking over approximately half of those, at a line-up of locomotives which it might be argued, represented a good cross section of the locomotives allocated to Nine Elms in BR days. From right to left we have glimpses of: M7; N; 'Lord Nelson'; BR Std. Class 5; E4; and a 'West Country' Pacific.**

Title page: **Drummond T9 No.30707 of 1899 vintage stands outside its home shed at Eastleigh soaking up the evening sunlight on 18th April 1956 as the fireman tends to the coal situation on the tender. The engine shed here was some four years younger than the 4-4-0 but was looking much older. However, whereas locomotives received an overhaul every few years or so, engine sheds were not so lucky hence the somewhat dilapidated state of 71A's north end gable; refurbishment, however, was not far away as British Railways mustered the funds to finance the rebuilding of dozens of its engine sheds throughout the country. Eastleigh though was to get a simple re-cladding with corrugated materials and no glass – cheap and cheerful! The fifteen road building was of the through type, which enabled a fair number of the 120 plus locomotives allocated at this time, to stable under cover. On this Wednesday in April 1956, that requirement does not appear to have arisen with few engines at home.**

Printed and bound by The Amadeus Press, Cleckheaton, West Yorkshire
First published in the United Kingdom by Book Law Publications, 382 Carlton Hill, Nottingham, NG4 1JA

STEWARTS LANE

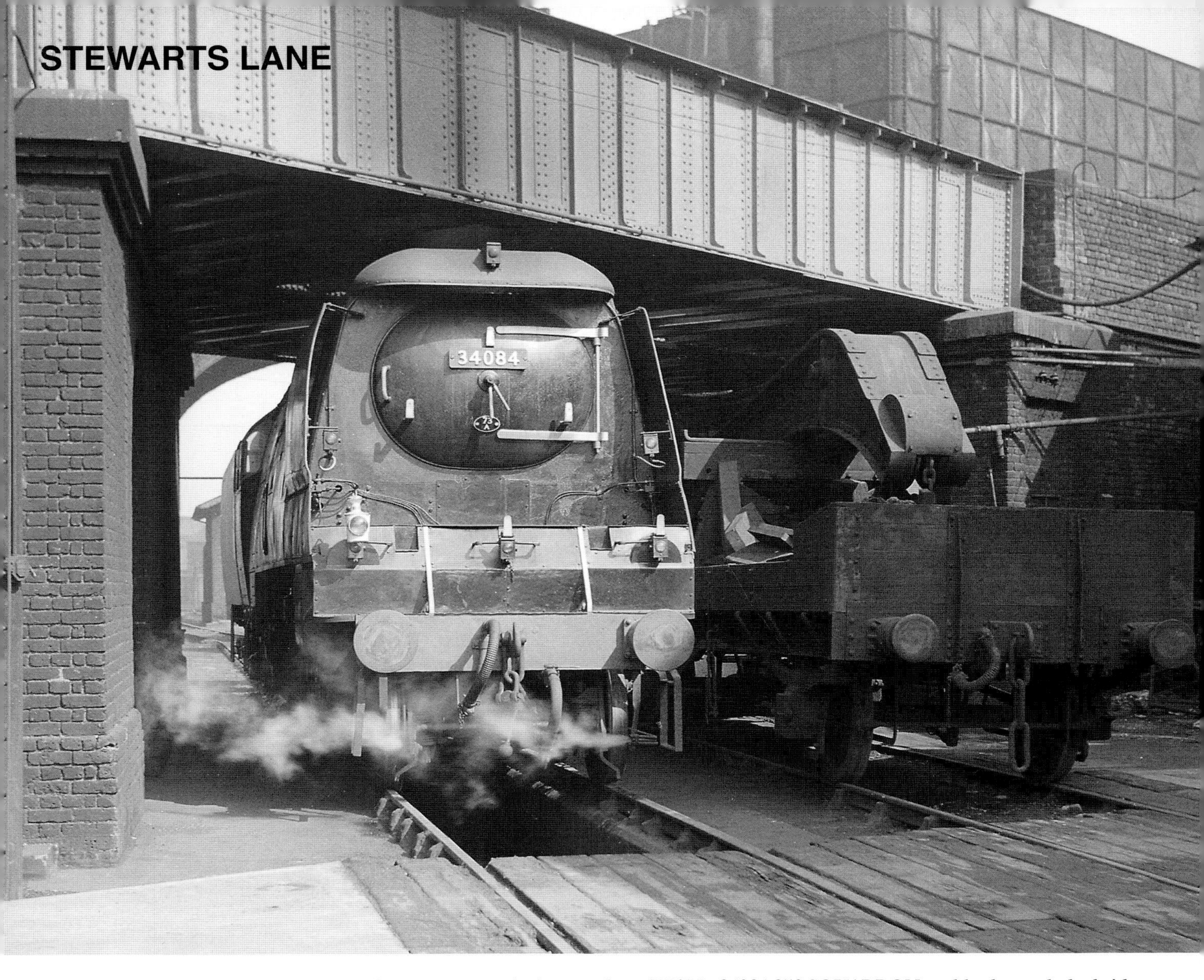

With Stewarts Lane steam breakdown crane for company, a nicely turned-out 'BB' No.34084 253 SQUADRON, stables beneath the bridge carrying the Factory Junction to Longhedge Junction line over the western section of the shed yard on the afternoon of Tuesday 1st April 1958. Although allocated new to 73A in November 1948, the Pacific had transferred to Ramsgate in May 1951 and had just been re-allocated to Stewarts Lane one month prior to this scene being recorded on film. It was fortunate that the 'BB' was captured here because ten days later No.34084 moved on to Dover, which was to be its last home on the Eastern Section before a permanent transfer to the Western Section in November 1960. Judging by the amount of staining on the bridge parapet above the locomotive, and the lack of such on the girder above the crane, it would appear that the breakdown crane was stabled at this location regularly.

At the other end of the shed yard, on that same afternoon in April 1958, Stirling 'O1' class 0-6-0 No.31064 is topped up with water prior to working off shed. This former South Eastern Railway engine was built at Ashford in November 1896, the class being Stirling's first design for the SER. It had transferred to Stewarts Lane from Ashford just twelve months before this scene was captured and had obviously not been cleaned during that period. However, it was not long for this world anyway and by the end of the month would be en route back to Ashford – the locomotive works this time – where it was condemned on arrival and cut up with almost indecent haste! Note the pile of ash and clinker near the front end of the 0-6-0; the fire, ashpan and smokebox cleaning area was on the other side of the yard!

Four separate routes passed Stewarts Lane engine shed, each one offering a different, if somewhat brief aspect of the yard. Any enthusiasts on the train crossing the viaduct in the background on this 19th day of September 1956 – a Wednesday – would probably get the best grandstand view but that was all; the chances of seeing any locomotive numbers were virtually nil, as their train accelerated away from Victoria on its journey south. Even those with binoculars would not be able to spot the number of the diminutive P class 0-6-0T No.31325 because its smokebox was facing the wrong way! The six-coupled tank was seemingly rostered to be the shed pilot today, however, it is wearing a 75A Brighton shedplate so presumably No.31325 was actually on loan to Stewarts Lane or was perhaps en route to main works for overhaul. The engine was wearing a mixture of graffiti and 'extras' on its front end, amongst the latter was a motor vehicle registration plate DXP ?78, and another but unidentifiable plate placed above the smokebox numberplate! Just behind the P can be seen the depot's ash crane, another steam driven antique which was so important to the depot, its value could not be underestimated.

Class L1 4-4-0 has just come onto Stewarts Lane shed with an unidentified 'WC' Pacific after working the Up *NIGHT FERRY* into Victoria on Tuesday morning, 1st day of November 1955. The overnight working was usually very heavy and required double-heading throughout hence the Dover supplied 4-4-0. Although sunshine is trying to brighten the winter gloom, it would be fighting a losing battle with the ever present menace of fog which, in those post-war days especially, managed to slow the pace of life throughout the country as transport especially was disrupted, not least the railways. It would be interesting to know if the L1 worked back home on a balancing turn or did it double-head the next Down working of the continental sleeper.

The steam-age importance of the so-called boat trains insofar as travel between Britain and the rest of Europe was concerned cannot be understated. Nowadays air travel and indeed the Chunnel itself have put those heady days of international connections into a league of their own. Yes, the ferries still ply their trade but heavy road vehicles and holidaymakers in their own cars make up the cargo now with not a steel tyre in sight. It was a different age and a very different world in 1958 when the *GOLDEN ARROW* was probably the most important working on the Southern Region and the locomotives used to power it to and from Dover/Folkestone were amongst the best maintained and the smartest looking. 'Britannia' No.70014 IRON DUKE (someone certainly had a sense of humour – or was it devilment – transferring that particular Pacific to 73A for the duty) is preparing to reverse off shed and down to Victoria on Tuesday 1st April 1958 with the full regalia bestowed on the train engine of that particular Pullman which was variously known as Stewarts Lane Duty No.4. No.70014 was one of a pair of 'Brits' sent to Stewarts Lane in September 1951, No.70004 being the other, particularly to work the boat trains. Both engines, and indeed the Pullman stock, had a fairly easy time of it at 73A as the *GA*, for instance, was worked Down to Folkestone, light engine to Dover with the stock following later, then the whole ensemble worked back from Dover later the same afternoon! Of course other duties were undertaken by the Pacifics including the occasional trip on the Western section on a Nine Elms job. Towards the end of June 1958 the 'pampered pair' left Stewarts Lane, and indeed the Southern, for a much more arduous life on the London Midland Region – all things must pass!

BASINGSTOKE

Even though it had lost its 70D coding status in March 1963, Basingstoke became one of the last operational engine sheds on the Southern Region and was still servicing steam locomotives into July 1967. Ten years earlier, on 17th April 1957, one of the oldest surviving Urie N15s – the 'King Arthurs' – and in fact the last of the class with Bulleid multiple jet blastpipe and large diameter chimney, No.30755 THE RED KNIGHT, stables by the old coaling stage with the morning sun light reflecting off its flanks. This locomotive had just days left before it was called into works and condemned! Basingstoke had a number of these 4-6-0s allocated, Nos.30748, 30749, 30750, and 30751 all followed our subject here to the scrapheap during that summer of 1957 whilst No.30738 managed to hang on until the following February. The shed was also home to the last of the N15X, No.32331 which was a casualty of June 1957.

One of the Maunsell 1925-built 'King Arthurs' No.30455 SIR LANCELOT, from Nine Elms shed, makes its way from the modern covered coaling stage and on to the shed on 17th April 1957 to await a working which would take it home. The eight wheel tender suited this class perfectly, the proportions giving the locomotive a powerful yet graceful look. This particular 'Arthur' transferred from London to Basingstoke at the end of the summer timetable and actually ended its days here along with many other 4-6-0s; was the proximity of Eastleigh works the reason why so many of these engines were transferred to 70D?

The yard on the north side of Basingstoke shed on the evening of Saturday 31st August 1963 with two Western Region engines, a 'Grange' and a 61XX tank stabled with the local motive power in the shape of U class No.31638, actually from Guildford, and a BR Standard. Both of the WR engines would have worked through from Reading and though unidentified, neither were probably strangers to this inter-regional motive power changeover point. The 70ft turntable was just to the right of the photograph, out of frame, and the WR 4-6-0 had already used the appliance to be ready for its homeward working, whenever that occurred; note that the 'Grange' is *still* carrying its nameplates.

En route to Eastleigh for works, C Class 0-6-0 No.31150 pauses at Basingstoke in company with a Q1 on 14th October 1961. The less than presentable former SECR engine is nearing its sixtieth birthday but would never reach that milestone as it was broken up at Eastleigh shortly after arrival. As for the Q1 which it had picked up whilst working over from Dover, and was probably not in steam, that was obviously going for overhaul as none of that forty-strong class were withdrawn until 1963.

A favourite place for spotters' to spend the day by the main line at Basingstoke was on the embankment at the back – station end – of the engine shed. Witness the pair enjoying the spring sunshine on 17th April 1957 as 'WC' No.34106 LYDFORD runs past as it arrives at Basingstoke with a Southampton (Terminus)-Waterloo semi-fast. This aspect of the engine shed offers a view of the rear wall with its near greenhouse effect gable! What's more, the windows appear clean but that might be a trick of the late morning sunlight. Basingstoke shed opened in 1905 as a replacement for another much smaller shed located south of the main line which was removed during the alterations and enlargement of the passenger station. Although, in effect, closed twice by British Railways, in 1963 and finally in July 1967, demolition could only take place once and that event occurred in 1969 but by then the spotters' would not have required that embankment any more because steam had disappeared from this part of the world some two years previously.

Typical motive power during the final years! BR Standard Cl.4 mixed traffic tender engine No.75075, one of the double-chimney versions, is prepared for duty at Basingstoke on 10th September 1966. At this time the 4-6-0 was allocated to Eastleigh shed though it is difficult to tell on first glance. For the Standard this kind of event at Basingstoke was just like old times because No.75075 had spent two and a half years allocated to 70D from June 1956 to January 1959 when it transferred to Three Bridges. After working from various sheds on that section of the SR, it returned to the Western section in December 1963 which proved to be its final move. Like all the active members of the Region's steam fleet in July 1967, it was withdrawn, aged eleven and a bit! Of course, this wasn't the only Standard 4 to be allocated to Basingstoke during those times of transition when the older designs were giving way to BR's own trade mark locomotive fleet. Besides No.75075 arriving during that summer of 1956, so did class mates Nos.75076 to 75079. Others followed – 75074 in 1957, 75065 to 75067 in November 1962. They were useful engines and well liked by the enginemen. Fifteen of the class were allocated new to the Southern and all had the larger BR1B tenders which were not equipped with water pick-up gear but had a capacity of 4725 gallons. Amongst the duties performed by the Basingstoke – and later the Eastleigh engines sub-shedded at Basingstoke – were the semi-fast passenger services to Waterloo and Salisbury, besides the Portsmouth-Cardiff, and Brighton-Plymouth trains. On the right can be seen the corridor tender of a very important visitor to the shed on this day, FLYING SCOTSMAN. It is nice to see the crew looking dapper in their light coloured clothing – for now, at least!

Our final view of Basingstoke takes us back to Saturday 31st August 1963 and shows the western aspect of the shed with a virtual full-house which is almost entirely made up of former Southern designs. Feltham based S15 No.30840 is just making its way onto the shed in the evening after having worked in on a heavy freight. Others visible include two more S15s, Nos.30830 and 30837, Standard No.76067, and a U Class mogul. The proximity of the busy station is evident from this angle. A last reminder of what used to be the norm at Basingstoke was seen shortly after this event was recorded when 'WC' No.34002 SALISBURY passed through the station heading west and into history with a long train of six-wheel milk tank empties. Much could be discussed about the BR of the 60s and 70s wanting to rid itself of certain traffic in a move which, with hindsight, was nothing more than financial suicide; the milk traffic was one such unwanted commodity, fish was another. No doubt we could go on!

FELTHAM

The low morning sun highlights certain occupants of Feltham shed on Sunday 9th December 1962. For some reason I failed to identify the Q1; perhaps their commonality about the place allowed the slip of the pen in favour of engines belonging to fast receding classes. S15 No.30511 has its motion down but was not a victim of withdrawal – that event was well over a year away – and was merely waiting its turn to be pushed back into the one-road repair shop for further attention. On the shed yard, beyond the 4-6-0, a regular visitor from Hither Green, 'W' No.31922, was taking a break prior working back home with yet another cross-London freight. Feltham engine shed had been built purely to house the freight locomotives which served the nearby marshalling yard and had been brought into use by the L&SWR on the eve of Grouping in 1922 but was not fully operational until 1923. However, Feltham became something of a trend-setter in engine shed terms, especially for the Southern Railway. The use of concrete in the building's construction is evident and it was from this, then revolutionary, material that the Southern chose to build six new engine sheds over the next decade. By 1962 Feltham shed was looking worn out, the glass in the northlight roof was slowly disappearing but more importantly, the concrete itself was crumbling from the affects of the corrosive combination of steam locomotive exhaust and rain water. Luckily for BR the end of steam was nigh and the requirement to replace the shed did not exist after closure in 1967.

Three withdrawn H16 class Pacific tanks lie abandoned alongside the lofty south wall of the repair shop at Feltham on Sunday 9th December 1962. Nos.30516 and 30520 are identifiable. This class consisted of just five engines, all allocated to Feltham since their introduction between November 1921 and February 1922, until February 1960 when Nos.30516 and 30517 transferred to Eastleigh and worked that area for a while prior to returning to Feltham. The class was built specifically to work the inter-regional freight traffic between the yards at Feltham and the LMS yards in north London but they did undertake other work and one of them could be seen on a daily basis working a filling-in turn hauling empty stock between Waterloo and Clapham Junction after working in on a freight from Feltham. All five were withdrawn in November 1962 and subsequently broken up. On the extreme left of the picture is Stanier 8F No.48671 of Wellingborough which had probably worked in on a coal train from the LM Region.

Besides the big tanks of Class H16, Feltham also housed a healthy number of S15 4-6-0s – twenty-five and more – for the longer distance express goods traffic. No.30501 was one of that batch for many years and is seen immobile at the south end of the shed on 21st January 1956 in the two-tone livery of jet black and filth. Just discernible on that tender is the very small version of the BR emblem which was placed quite high on the tender side and not looking quite right but note, it was in line with the locomotive number on the cabside. Built in June 1920 at Eastleigh under the Urie regime, the class was expanded in 1927 and again in 1936 but most of the original LSWR engines were allocated to Feltham whilst the two Southern batches were shared between Exmouth Junction, Salisbury and Feltham; although in BR days Redhill gained three of the 1927 batch transferred from Feltham. No.30501 was one of half a dozen of the Feltham engines condemned in June 1963.

A somewhat surprising visitor to Feltham shed on that Saturday 21st January 1956 was 'King Arthur' No.30774 SIR GAHERIS, a fairly recent transfer from Stewarts Lane to Nine Elms. It can only be assumed that the N15 had worked in on a freight train. Note that its eight-wheel bogie tender is lined and has the BR emblem placed centrally, between the lining. Although five years younger than the S15 just featured, the North British built engine had spent much of its life on the Eastern Section of the SR and was somewhat surplus to requirements on the Western Section. Already by this date the class had been broken up by the first withdrawals; No.30774's turn for the chop occurred in January 1960. In the summer of 1959 Feltham became home for a couple of the 1925-built 'Scotch Arthurs' but both of those had gone by August 1960, one for scrapping, the other on transfer to Basingstoke.

PLYMOUTH FRIARY

The Ivatt Cl.2 tank engine represents the last type of motive power to be allocated to the former Southern Region engine shed at Plymouth Friary. Coded 72D by British Railways, Friary was subordinate to Exmouth Junction but in 1958 the Western Region took over and Friary became the first of the former L&SWR sheds in the West Country to be transferred to the WR. The fact that the shed was located deep within the Newton Abbot motive power division virtually within a stones throw of Laira shed yet under the control of 72A made no apparent sense economically so it was inevitable that common sense would eventually prevail and Exmouth Junction surrender one of its far flung assets. More radical regional boundary changes, affecting SR assets west of Salisbury, would follow but that particular event was some five years into the future. Meanwhile, Friary, whose allocation comprised about a dozen locomotives in 1958 – all tank engines – became 83H until it was closed in May 1963. The first Ivatt 2-6-2T allocated to Friary, No.41315, arrived in Plymouth during the first months of 1953 on transfer from Exmouth Junction; although three others' all out-stationed from Exmouth Junction to work the Callington branch, where stabled and maintained at Friary between turns. No.41315 was to remain the sole member of its class actually allocated to 72D until November 1956 when Nos.41314 (ex Bricklayers Arms) and 41316 (ex Ashford) arrived at Friary. A month later No.41314 returned to London, swapped for No.41302. It was possible that No.41314 never made the trip to the West Country and may well have been in works; its return to the 'Brick' requiring a balancing transfer to Plymouth by No.41302. The Friary quartet was finally completed during the spring of 1957 when No.41317 transferred from Ashford. So, for the next six years, the Ivatt tanks watched the Friary allocation dwindle until they alone were left to make the final transfer to Laira in 1963. This is a smart looking No.41316 seen outside the east end of the shed on 29th August 1957. Note that it still wears the Ashford shedplate some ten months after its 'official' transfer to 72D.

B4 No.30102 was one of four 0-4-0T attached to Friary shed for working the Southern Region dock branches around Plymouth during BR days. Originally working at Southampton docks, this particular four-coupled tank had been replaced by a 'USA' tank during the immediate post-war years, so was therefore a relative 'newcomer' to the West Country compared to other B4s at Friary. No.30102 had been, until ousted from its job at Southampton, named GRANVILLE in line with other B4 tanks which carried the names of French or Channel Island ports served at one time or another by the LSWR shipping fleet. Built at Nine Elms in December 1893, this engine worked for British Railways until the ripe old age of seventy years! It now enjoys a life in preservation. Contrast the lined bunker of O2 No.30182 stabled in front, and No.30102's own drab livery; the difference, at that time - 31st March 1956 - between those engines which worked passenger trains and those that did not! The spark arrester indicates that the 0-4-0T was probably working the timber yards and creosote installation at Oreston but the other B4s allocated to Friary – some had been at the shed since arriving new in the 1890s albeit to the original shed by the station – worked the likes of the Cattewater harbour branch where petro-chemical installations also required the use of spark arresters. The Turnchapel branch to the east – which gave access to the Oreston yards – and the Stonehouse Pool branch just south of Devonport (Kings Road), also provided regular work for the Friary 0-4-0Ts.

The main line from Plymouth's former Southern Railway passenger and goods stations at Friary, to the rest of the world, ran alongside the northern boundary of the engine shed of the same name – note the tank engine and attached brakevan on the left, standing at the shed throat. Around midday on Thursday 29th August 1957 a rather heavy Plymouth (Friary)-London (Waterloo) express has just left the terminus behind Nine Elms allocated 'WC' No.34030 WATERSMEET, which, it might be said, looks nicely spruced-up. Once past the shed the train would deviate left at Friary Junction, pass Laira engine shed, join the WR main line at Lipson Junction, and then head west through North Road station to Devonport Junction where the SR was rejoined for the long and winding road to Exeter! Being one of the depots located at the western extremity of the Southern system, Friary naturally attracted a small number of the lightweight Pacifics for working trains such as this – looking at the formation of the train perhaps two 'WC' should be at the head! Shortly after Nationalisation, BR stationed a number of West Country Pacifics at Friary over the following ten years; one of those engines, appropriately, being No.34003 PLYMOUTH. In complete contrast to the train illustrated, the Plymouth portion of the *DEVON BELLE* would often arrive at Friary station with just two coaches in it's consist, behind a 'WC'; the same could be said of the Plymouth portion of the '*ACE*'! On the left, between the shed yard and the main line is the one-time branch to Plymstock, Turnchapel and Yealmpton which remains open to this day, though only in part, serving private sidings.

Shortly after the London express had cleared the route on that August 1957 Thursday, another 'West Country', No.34021 DARTMOOR headed a freight bound for Exeter. Which route the freight train took is unknown but SR enginemen often worked over the WR mainline via Newton Abbot to keep route knowledge up-to-date in case of any possible diversions, which it might be added were not infrequent. It was not unusual to see the Pacifics hauling freight over the route between Plymouth and Exeter via Okehampton because Friary had no other suitable motive power and 2-6-0 tender engines, for instance, from Exmouth Junction were not always available. Although Friary shed had hosted the first lightweight Pacifics since late 1945 when Exmouth Junction sent them with expresses from Waterloo, it wasn't until April 1948 that the shed received its own allocation of 'WC' Pacifics. A listing of the engines involved over that decade might be of interest thus:

34003 PLYMOUTH	April 1948 to 20th May 1950 and 17th June to 9th September 1950.
34011 TAVISTOCK	April 1948 to 11th April 1951.
34012 LAUNCESTON	April 1948 to 8th December 1950.
34013 OKEHAMPTON	April 1948 to 12th May 1951.
34021 DARTMOOR	April 1948 to 8th December 1950.
34032 CAMELFORD	20th March to 12th May 1951.
34033 CHARD	6th October to 6th December 1951.
34034 HONITON	8th December 1950 to 19th March 1952.
34035 SHAFTESBURY	8th December 1950 to 14th January 1958.
34036 WESTWARD HO	8th December 1950 to 14th January 1958.
34037 CLOVELLY	12th May 1951 to 14th January 1958.
34038 LYNTON	12th May 1951 to 14th January 1958.

It will be noticed that, tidily, the first engines listed numerically were the first allocated whilst the last, became the last! The loss of its charges was really only a book exercise because Friary shed, as mentioned earlier, had become part of the WR by now (83H), but the Pacifics kept visiting Plymouth (Friary station closed in September 1958 and passenger services were diverted to North Road station whilst goods traffic continued to be handled at Friary) and coming to Friary shed for servicing; right up to its closure in 1963. Even the Rebuilt examples of the 'WC/BB' class, which had originally been banned from working west of Exeter, could, from 1960, work the Plymouth road at least. It might be added that Friary engine shed never had a turntable capable of turning the Pacifics so they had to venture out to the triangles at either Cattewater or at Lipson. On shed, and taking water, can be seen another of the depot's quartet of Ivatt tanks.

BRIGHTON

On Sunday 13th April 1958 the Railway Correspondence & Travel Society ran a special train from London (Victoria) to Newhaven with H2 class No.32424 BEACHY HEAD as the motive power. The occasion was to be the 'Last Brighton Atlantic Farewell' special. However, not only was No.32424 running as the last LBSCR Atlantic, it was also, by now, the last operational Atlantic on British Railways! Still only forty-seven years old, the 4-4-2 was one of six of a class attributed to D.E.Marsh which he had developed from his earlier H1 class. The six were built at Brighton between June 1911 and January 1912 and the first of the class to be withdrawn was No.(3)2423 in May 1949 before it received it BR number. Four of the remaining five were condemned during August and October 1956 leaving our subject to soldier on alone. Marsh's other five Atlantics of Class H1 – which were near enough copies of Ivatt's Great Northern Railway C1 Atlantics – had all gone by July 1951. Surprisingly, at the time, and especially nowadays, BEACHY HEAD was condemned and soon afterwards cut up. The Brighton Atlantics were no more. Perhaps the fact that the GNR C1 No.251 had already been preserved had tempered any notion within BR that a SR Atlantic should be saved. Here on that fateful Sunday, No.32424 backs onto Brighton shed after that farewell trip. Within a few weeks it would be scrapped!

Brighton engine shed on that memorable Sunday in April 1958 with No.32424 BEACHY HEAD as the star turn. Brighton shed had always hosted a wealth of SR types – some sixteen different classes in 1950 for instance – and on this particular day it still presented an excellent selection of locomotives. In view are: C2X, E4, K, L, M7, Ns of various types, Urie S15, WC/BB, BR Std. Cl.4. 350 h.p. DE shunters. Then there are the preserved engines represented by the LSWR T9 4-4-0 No.120 and A1X 0-6-0T BOXHILL which had been brought out for display. Blowing off in the middle distance can be seen 'King Arthur' No.30796 SIR DODINAS LE SAVAGE, which was waiting to haul the special back to London. The special consisted of seven carriages including a Pullman Buffet car on which 350 enthusiasts and friends travelled. In the far distance, on the viaduct, a diminutive A1X is returning from the morning session at Newhaven shed (*see* later).

32442
32475
31766
13219

The layout of Brighton engine shed was not one of the most efficient on British Railways and arguably it was probably amongst the least efficient regarding movement and egress. Obviously, its location, in the fork of two busy main lines, with the town's main passenger station platforms virtually sharing the same space as the depot's stabling roads, had some negative aspects. BR, and indeed the Southern Railway before them, had made the most of a bad situation and rather than spend vast amounts of money trying to modernise the shed (when that money didn't really exist anyway for much of the time that steam locomotives worked the S.Reg.) the minimum was spent to modernise facilities as befitted the situation. This illustration reveals something of the coaling area on the west side of the shed yard on 7th October 1962 with E6 No.32417 and K No.32341 each waiting their turn. The coaling platform, with its cantilevered shelter was served by the crane just showing its jib above the wagons. It was a far cry from the mechanical coaling plants present at most other important motive power centres but the staff at 75A managed to service their engines to the end without so much as a groan. The two locomotives in the frame, both Brighton allocated engines, would be condemned by the end of the year so that, at least, would be two less to worry about!

A partially clean E4, No.32508, stables on the shed roads behind the works at Brighton on 13th April 1958. Already fifty-eight years old, the Brighton built tank does not have much longer for this world but it will reach its sixtieth birthday! The ramshackle nature of the wall of the building behind the engine suggests piecemeal and temporary repairs, a reflection perhaps of British Railways as a whole. Meanwhile the six-coupled tank, after a spell in works, appears ready to have its fire lit first thing Monday morning.

The last of the Drummond LSWR D15 4-4-0s, No.30465 of Nine Elms shed, stands at the side of Brighton engine shed on 11th January 1956 waiting for the call which would take it into the adjacent works for scrapping.

***Opposite Page*: A1X No.32636 *(above)* takes water at Brighton shed on 7th October 1962; the stature of the locomotive makes the fireman holding the bag, appear like a giant! *(below)* Being coupled to E6 No.32418, the A1X is prepared to back off shed to take up a working to Seaford, and then onto Newhaven (Town) and shed with the RCTS *SUSSEX SPECIAL* rail tour.**

32636
DP
32636
30929
ALVERN
32636
32418
32418

EASTLEIGH

In order to re-use probably the most expensive component of a motor train combination, Urie rebuilt the 2-2-0T locomotive sections of the three surviving Nine Elms-built Drummond LSWR motor trains between 1913 and 1923. This trio became 0-4-0 tank engines and were classified C14, designated for shunting work; all were to be used in the Western Section of the SR. Of the three, one went to the Service Department working the sleeper depot at Redbridge until withdrawn as 77s in 1959, whilst the other two went to work shunting Southampton docks but by BR days had migrated to Eastleigh where they shunted the engine shed. This is No.30588 on 18th April 1956, the whereabouts of sister No.30589 unknown but it would not be too far away. Note the 0P rather than 0F power classification above the number. Also, observe the handrails and enlarged bottom footstep provided for the comfort of the shunters who worked alongside these little tank engines. No.30588 perhaps had something of a charmed life but that too came to an end in December 1957 when it was condemned. No.30589 had gone six months earlier but their Departmental sister, No.77s, continued working down the line at Redbridge until April 1959 when its boiler eventually gave up and, with no replacements available, the only option was condemnation and cutting up.

A respectable looking Rebuilt 'WC' No.34025 WHIMPLE has its tender replenished at Eastleigh on 14th October 1961. The Pacific was a fairly recent acquisition for 71A having been transferred from Bricklayers Arms at the end of the previous May. No.34025 was amongst the nine Lightweight Pacifics to be rebuilt in 1957 and it emerged from Eastleigh on 26th October – nearly four years to the day – as the fifth of the class to be dealt with. The rebuilding of the 'WC/BB' ended in May 1961, coinciding but in no way related to this engines' transfer to the Western section. Moving on to Bournemouth in October 1965, No.34025 managed to remain operational until the Southern Region called it a day with steam. Not amongst the twenty which were to be eventually preserved, it was later sold for scrap and cut up during 1968. Behind the 'WC' and looking not nearly as healthy, is a 'Lord Nelson' 4-6-0 which, as its appearance suggests, was nearing the end of its life. Note the semaphore signal attached to the gantry at the top of the water tower!

This view outside Eastleigh shed from 18th April 1956 shows the very first 'Merchant Navy' No.35001 CHANNEL PACKET in *almost* original condition. The Exmouth Junction Pacific had just arrived at Eastleigh shed prior to entry into the works for a General overhaul which included re-siting the safety valves and radical modifications to the tender when it was 'cut-down' to resemble what would be its final form. Entering the shops on 30th April, No.35001 emerged on 9th June still in this form; it was to be another three years before the class leader was to be rebuilt. A small number of these engines managed to stay with the same tenders throughout their lives; No.35001 nearly managed the feat with tender No.3111 but a leaking tank, amongst other things, during May 1941 saw 21C1 (its original Southern railway number) borrow tender No.3112 from 'not yet ready for traffic' sister No.21C2, whilst tender 3111 received the necessary repairs. Long after withdrawal in November 1964, No.35001 was coupled to another tender, prior to being towed to the private scrap yard which had purchased it.

Ex-works M7 No.30111 makes an impressive sight from this ground level angle which was captured at Eastleigh engine shed on 14th October 1961. The Bournemouth based 0-4-4T had just completed its last General overhaul which would see it through to withdrawal in January 1964. Note the corrugated cladding which is now covering the shed gable.

One year later on 11th November 1962, and one of the Beattie well tanks recently withdrawn from active service at Wadebridge, languishes on the shed yard at Eastleigh. The decision to withdraw the three '0298' class 2-4-0WT had been taken sometime in the previous twelve months and it was only a matter of time before their sixty-odd year job working the mineral branch up to Wenford Bridge was taken over by another, albeit suitable, class which turned out to by a former Great Western designed small Pannier tank! The trio of Beattie tanks were all, apparently, destined for preservation but it turned out that our subject here and No.30587 were the only ones to make it, No.30586 went instead for scrap in March 1964; perhaps it was the rectangular splashers carried by that engine which threw it out of favour!

Because of the narrow cab side sheets on the Beattie tanks, the SR had problems getting the five figure numbers into the available space. The solution was to use the same font for the figures as those used on the diesel shunters – Condensed Grotesque – which was, as the name implies, narrower. The cabside numbers were actually not much bigger than those on the smokebox numberplate. The small size of the locomotive enabled it to carry off the charade without any undue fuss. The British Railways crest was also on the small side note; this again was one of those made specifically for the diesel shunter fleets, basically the smallest available.

A battered, neglected and thoroughly run-down Adams '0415' class Atlantic tank resides at the buffer stops of the scrap line on 14th October 1961. This scene is probably reminiscent of Eastleigh yard during 1916 and the few years immediately afterwards when the switch-on of the L&SWR London suburban electrification made dozens of these handsome locomotives redundant. However, the South-Western' could not scrap them at the time because of the circumstances and prevailing conditions imposed by the wartime Government. Therefore, many of the 4-4-2T engines were simply stored outside with little or no preparation for the coming years of exposure to the elements. A few were sold off and the L&SWR themselves kept hold of some too but with the coming of Grouping, the chances of the majority ever being activated again was gone. From 1928 the Southern Railway kept two engines for working the Lyme Regis branch, a job for which these tank engines were totally suited and on which they took turns about on a weekly basis. This class had taken over the branch working in about 1913. After the end of hostilities in 1945, the SR realised that post-war recovery was going to bring more seasonal visitors than ever before to the Dorset branch line so in 1946 they took the unprecedented step of purchasing from the East Kent Railway a former classmate of the pair which had been sold to the Ministry of Munitions in 1917. The EKR had secured the '0415' in 1919 and had obviously looked after their charge. Hopefully they made a profit out of the arrangement with the Southern. Three engines of the '0415' class therefore entered BR ownership. All allocated to Exmouth Junction shed, the trio worked the branch to Lyme Regis from Axminster on a basis of one in steam working the branch with two spare although in summer there would be two working the branch with one spare. Shopping's was carried out over winter, with all three then available for the summer workings, including emergency cover – a perfect situation! And so things remained that way for thirteen years until the Western Region took over the branch in 1961. Even in nationalised industries there are those who become 'empire builders'. BR was no exception and probably had more than most! The Adams tanks were made redundant and their place taken by Ivatt 2MT 2-6-2T. The first of the Atlantic tanks to be condemned was No.30584, our subject here, which was withdrawn in February 1961 and was eventually cut up at the end of 1961. Of the other two, which were both withdrawn in July 1961, No.30582 followed No.30584 for scrap a few months later. No.30583 however, the former LSWR, M of M, EKR, and short-term Southern Railway charge, was purchased for preservation, the fifth time it had changed hands financially – which may be a record of sorts! They were handsome engines. Stripped of its numberplate and the Dubs & Co. works plates, the Radial tank has a duplication of numbers and BR emblem showing through the faded paintwork. Obviously, this engine did not receive the new BR crest so may not have received any major overhauls since the 1956/57 winter.

Another Adams 'old-timer' languishing in the scrap line at Eastleigh shed on that day in October 1961 was 'mainland' O2 No.30183. A long term resident of Plymouth Friary, the 0-4-4T had been condemned during the previous month after making its final journey to Eastleigh from its Devon retreat. Shed mate and sister No.30192 had preceded this engine to works and was broken up a few weeks beforehand. No.30183's turn for scrapping would come in November, leaving just two O2s at Plymouth. Those final two would make their way to Eastleigh in 1962 as the Southern Region influence was slowly eroded from the West of England.

It wasn't all doom and gloom at Eastleigh in 1961 or perhaps it was! L1 class No.31756 was something of a newcomer to 71A during the summer after being recently transferred from Nine Elms to which shed it had transferred during the previous summer after moving from Tonbridge on the South Eastern Section. The L1s were no strangers to Eastleigh or indeed the South Western Section either; in late 1952 four of them had been transferred to Eastleigh from Stewarts Lane in exchange for five L class 4-4-0s which had not made much of an impression with the Eastleigh footplatemen. Those Ls had arrived from Ashford and Ramsgate in January 1952 as part of a ten-engine posse which had ascended on 71A to apparently cover for an expected motive power shortage. In the summer of 1959 the Kent Coast electrification had caused numerous steam locomotives to be displaced and amongst those sent to Nine Elms were the remnants of the L and L1 classes. Within weeks of arriving at 71A, half of the L class had been withdrawn and a third of the L1s went shortly after Christmas. The condemnations continued to whittle down the two classes during 1960 and by the end of 1961 only one L1 remained – No.31786 which lasted until February 1962 and was quickly dispatched after withdrawal. Our subject here was withdrawn in October 1961.

Two locomotives which did have a future in front of them at Eastleigh in October 1961 were 'WC' No.34026 YES TOR and the unidentified but obviously ex-works Pannier tank behind the Pacific; Eastleigh was undertaking a number of PT repairs during this period. Note that the large dome cover on the 0-6-0PT appears like one of the radar randomes fitted to modern day warships. The Salisbury based 'West Country' had just completed a month-long Light Intermediate overhaul and was ready to return to traffic for another five years prior to withdrawal. The rather grotty looking BR Standard 9F at the end of the line may well have been a visitor off one of the Fawley-Bromford Bridge tank train workings or it too could be awaiting works attention because a large number of the class received various levels of repair at Eastleigh during this period.

It is amazing how the Southern Region, more than any other perhaps, relied so much on the BR Standard classes during the final dozen years of steam working. The SR Standards, which comprised tender engines from Class 4MT, both 2-6-0 and 4-6-0 versions, Class 5MT and eventually Class 9F, along with tank engines from classes 2, 3 and 4, could be found virtually anywhere on the region undertaking all kinds of work from the haulage of express passenger trains to working branch lines; the two 'Britannia's' mentioned earlier must also be included in the total too. Of the fifteen Class 4s delivered new to the Region during 1955, five went to the South Eastern Section at Dover with the balance all going to Exmouth Junction on the South Western'. Of course that situation changed with traffic patterns and by 1956 the 72A engines had dispersed to Basingstoke, Bath Green Park, and Eastleigh. The Central Section got three of the original fifteen in early 1959 from the Eastleigh and Basingstoke allocations. No.75068, pictured outside Eastleigh shed on 9th May 1964 after attending works, was by now allocated to 70D, its final shed before withdrawal in July 1967. Delivered to Dover in September 1955, this engine certainly made its way around the region during its short lifetime, going to Bournemouth in June 1959, Eastleigh in May 1961, Brighton in November 1962, Stewarts Lane in April 1963, Norwood Junction five months later and finally Eastleigh during December of that year. Some eventually left the region but most remained to the end. Standing behind is 'BB' No.34064 FIGHTER COMMAND which was also ex-works after a Light Intermediate overhaul. The Pacific was now on Eastleigh's strength but ended up at Salisbury in October 1965.

It looks very clean but its only rain soaked! Withdrawn 'Schools' No.30917 formerly ARDINGLEY stands in the yard at Eastleigh on 9th March 1963 waiting for the call to the breakers, just as the massacre had started to gain momentum.

Believed to be the last operational 'Schools', No.30926 REPTON stands alongside the Eastleigh coaling stage after heading a special from Waterloo on Sunday 11th November 1962. The following month, this V Class 4-4-0, along with sixteen classmates, was condemned. However, that was not the end of the story for No.30926. Unlike No.30917, which was broken up, our subject was preserved and joined sisters Nos.30925 CHELTENHAM and 30928 STOWE in being kept for posterity.

Helping No.30926 during its haulage of the last special of 11th November 1962 [SPL 15] was the preserved T9 No.120 (ex 30120) in full L&SWR livery, and complete with eight-wheel tender. The 4-4-0 double-headed and being lead engine, it carried the reporting number on the target board. In this view captured on Eastleigh shed, the T9 has just left the coaling stage. Note that signal again!

Back to 9th March 1963, and its time to look at a couple of Service locomotives which had arrived at Eastleigh for scrapping: DS683, an A1 which was ex-Lancing carriage works, and the last mainland G6 class 0-6-0T DS682, which was ex-Meldon quarry. The G6, which up to November 1960 when it had become a Service locomotive, had been No.30238 and was withdrawn in December 1962.

The last S15, No.30837, taking water at Eastleigh shed on the occasion of the *S15 COMMEMORATIVE RAIL TOUR* on 9th January 1966 which was organised by the Locomotive Club of Great Britain. The nicely turned-out 4-6-0 had been withdrawn during the previous September along with the other remaining four members of the class. For some reason, although withdrawn, the S15 was allowed to haul the rail tour which encompassed a run from Waterloo to Eastleigh via Alton and the Mid-Hants. Line and return. The special was repeated a week later, but this time in the snow! After the event No.30837 was put back into store and eventually scrapped. Curiously, seven other members of the class found their way into preservation!

Dramatic natural lighting aids the man-made variety inside the engine shed at Eastleigh on 18th April 1964 to highlight Q class 0-6-0 No.30548 which was resting during a service pause of another LCGB special working. Named *THE HAMPSHIRE VENTURER RAIL TOUR*, the itinerary saw the 0-6-0 starting the tour at Portsmouth and continuing on via Andover, Salisbury and Poole. Hardly looking its best in this pose, the Q had probably benefited from that stream of sunlight coming from the opening in the roof but the railtour itself did nothing to immortalise the engine, nor indeed any of its class; No.30548 was withdrawn a year later and cut up shortly afterwards. Considering that these engines were the last from the Maunsell camp, none were preserved!

Surrounded by withdrawn locomotives, BR Standard Cl.4 No.80142 hurries down the shed roads outside the back of Eastleigh shed on 6th December 1964. If such a thing was possible, it could be construed that the eight-year old engine had been seized by a panic-attack and with its tank filler cap still open, it was trying to flee the scene of dead and discarded locomotives and return to its home shed at 75B Redhill. In June 1965 the Class 4 was itself put into storage when it was transferred to Salisbury. However, it was not withdrawn and remained in store until moved to Eastleigh in February 1966 where, just days later, on 3rd March, No.80142 was condemned! Some five months short of its tenth birthday, the 2-6-4T went to the wrong scrapyard in Wales; those of its class which ended up at Barry, rather than Bridgend, were saved by enthusiasts.

This view of BR Standard Cl.4 No.80012 is included simply because it was the last member of its class to receive a General overhaul and, at Eastleigh too. Here on shed on the 9th May 1964, barely days after being put back into traffic, the Cl.4 has a USA tank for company as fire cleaning is performed. At the time of this photograph, No.80012 was allocated to Feltham shed of all places and when it returned to 70B, it was joined by another Cl.4, No.80018. By the end of 1964 both of those Feltham tanks had joined the Eastleigh allocation. No.80012 moved back to London in October 1965 but this time it went to Nine Elms shed. Travelling companion No.80018 was not so fortunate and whilst at Eastleigh it was condemned in April 1965 and sold for scrap in the following August. Meanwhile, our subject settled in at 70A amongst the ever growing mounds of ash, clinker, and dead locomotives. Withdrawn in March 1967, it was towed down to Salisbury engine shed (which became a sort of showroom for scrap merchants) where, in August, it was sold to a yard in South Wales – Newport to be exact.

BOURNEMOUTH

Staying on the South-Western' for the time being, we venture down to Bournemouth where on Wednesday 18th April 1956 we meet a real working T9 in the shape of No.30304. Already fifty-six years old, the 4-4-0 had just seventeen months of operational life left before being called in for scrapping at Eastleigh. The T9 had been a Salisbury engine for much of its BR career and that was still its home when photographed at 71B on a glorious spring evening. Note the six-wheel tender which was one of only a dozen or so examples attached to engines in this class.

On that same April evening in 1956 the shed pilot was this grotty B4, No.30087, which was minus a shedplate. This engine had also spent most of its BR life allocated to one depot which in this case was Bournemouth. At the time of my visit, Bournemouth had another B4 allocated in the shape of No.30093. For reasons unknown, 71B required two of these little tank engines and when No.30087 was withdrawn in December 1958, No.30102 from Eastleigh took its place. That situation remained until April 1960 when, with the withdrawal of No.30093, and having just two others left in the class, No.30102 became the sole example at Bournemouth. By then diesel shunters had arrived on the premises and classes clinging on to existence, such as the B4s, were all but finished. However, No.30102 clung on until September 1963 becoming the penultimate B4 working on British Railways; No.30096 became the final member by a matter of days. Preservation called for both of those Nine Elms-built four-coupled tanks. No.30087 was, alas, scrapped shortly after withdrawal. Note the breakdown crane and its runner which, no doubt, the 0-4-0T would position near to the shed exit road ready for a more able bodied locomotive to haul to any incident.

TUNBRIDGE WELLS WEST

The former LB&SCR engine shed at Tunbridge Wells West was opened in 1890 to replace a smaller shed which was situated on the south side of the station in an area which later became sidings. In 1955 BR re-roofed the four-road shed using reclaimed rails and corrugated asbestos cladding; this re-roofing method was employed by BR at a number of sheds on the Southern, Bournemouth being another example. At midday on Saturday 23rd December 1961 the shed roof appears to be still in pristine condition as visiting BR Standard Cl.4 No.80064 simmers in the winter sunshine before working back home to Tonbridge. Of course, Tunbridge Wells had some Cl.4 Standard tanks of its own – ten new examples, Nos.80010 to 80019, were allocated to the shed during the summer and autumn of 1951 – with six of the original allocation from 1951 still resident. These had been joined by others from the end of November 1959 when SR based Fairburn 2-6-4Ts, including the half dozen at Tunbridge Wells West, were exchanged for London Midland based Standards; Nos.80095, 80137, 80138, 80139, 80140, 80141, and 80142. Many of the Std. Cl.4s stayed at Tunbridge Wells West until the shed lost its independent status, and 75F code, to become a sub-shed of Brighton on 9th September 1963. Final closure took place in June 1965. Note the lack of a 73J shedplate on No.80064.

23rd December 1961 again, with H class No.31544 reversing into the engine shed after a spell of duty on passenger work. With No.80064 beside it, the 0-4-4T reveals the only two classes of steam motive power working passenger duties in the area at this time. No.31544 remained at Tunbridge Wells until the shed became a Brighton sub at which time it was condemned and sent for scrap. Although not totally evident from this angle, the 'H' had been fitted with push-pull equipment in June 1954.

Collision imminent! No, not really. 'H' No.31005 moves down the shed yard and passes sister No.31518 at right angles on the turntable in this 1st June 1962 view. By 1959 seven of these 0-4-4Ts were allocated to 75F. The illustration allows us to see a couple of the locomotive facilities available at Tunbridge Wells West with one of the ever present Cl.4 Standard tanks standing alongside the primitive but effective coaling crane which, for a depot of this size, was adequate. The wooded background lends a rural atmosphere to the depot.

An interior view of Tunbridge Wells West shed showing the austere roof construction. The old rails and the soot blackened cladding contrasting nicely with white-washed walls! This undated photograph reveals three residents, only one of which is identified. The 'H' was allocated until July 1963 when it was condemned; the Std. Cl.4 could have been any one of fourteen which were allocated at one time or another, or indeed another from elsewhere. The M7 may well have been a Brighton engine which had worked in or perhaps was on loan from the parent shed. However, it has a NOT TO BE MOVED sign affixed to its bunker which adds to the mystery.

NEWHAVEN

Brighton Atlantic No.32424 BEACHY HEAD stands on the shed yard at Newhaven after its RCTS Farewell Special run from Victoria to Newhaven (Harbour) on 13th April 1958 (see also Brighton) which carried a *SUSSEX COAST LIMITED* headboard. The reason that particular route was chosen for the special run, was to enact the Atlantics' normal working routine which would often see it heading one of the Victoria-Newhaven boat trains. With enthusiasts taking photographs and notes, the other motive power on shed was not ignored; along with the two A1Xs, BR Std. Cl.4 No.80154 (the last locomotive built at Brighton incidentally) and a Ramsgate based 'Schools' No.30910 MERCHANT TAYLORS were also resident on this Sunday. The BR 2-6-4T hauled the special on the Newhaven (Town) to Brighton leg. Enthusiasts on the Bluebell Railway are nowadays building a replica of a Brighton Atlantic which just goes to reinforce the notion that an opportunity was certainly missed in 1958 to secure the last of the H2 class engines. The engine shed here was opened in 1887. It was built to replace a much earlier and smaller establishment located adjacent to Newhaven (Harbour) station, and which dated from 1847. British Railways re-roofed the four-road shed during the earliest days of Nationalisation, corrugated asbestos being once more the cladding of choice. A sub shed of Brighton, Newhaven never had a code of its own in BR days but closure took place on 9th September 1963 in line with other engines sheds in the Brighton district.

On that same Sunday, a couple of A1X 0-6-0Ts, Nos.32636 and 32640, joined in with the celebrations. Here, standing on the spur to the Railway wharf, alongside the 60ft turntable and the adjacent engineering shop, the pair hold court with the celebrity Atlantic whilst their respective crews, and enthusiasts alike, inspect and admire them all. Only No.32640 was actually involved with the special; it hauled the seven coach train away from Harbour station and up to Newhaven (Town) station. Note that both of the tank engines have different coal bunkers; No.32636 has a slightly taller bunker – with just inches in it – whilst No.32640 has a longer bunker. Consequently, the longer bunker accepts normal size numbers, whereas the tall but short bunker on 32636 requires the modified numbers known as Condensed Grotesque. From this angle it is easy to see the difference between the two sets of figures.

Four and a half years on and A1X No.32636 is still at Newhaven and is seen taking water from the shed column on Sunday 7th October 1962, having headed the RCTS *SUSSEX SPECIAL* rail tour with E6 No.32412 from Brighton. On shed this day was an E4 No.32479, E6 No.32418, A1X No.32670, and a 350 h.p. 0-6-0DE shunter which is just visible inside the building. This 0-6-0T was, at that time, the oldest locomotive working on British Railways.

NINE ELMS

Outside the 'New shed' at Nine Elms on 28th November 1964, a respectable looking and unrebuilt 'WC' No.34019 BIDEFORD, along with an unidentified Rebuilt 'Merchant Navy', add scale to the mechanical coaling plant. The engine shed itself was a large structure, not just in width and length, but in volume, its lofty roof giving smoke a chance to escape to atmosphere before choking personnel at ground level. This particular shed was built in 1910, the 'Old shed' dated from 1885. However, the 'New shed' had replaced a semi-roundhouse building, once located on the far side of the coaling plant, which was somewhat unique in having twin turntables, each serving approximately fourteen radiating roads – what a sight that must have been before it closed in 1909! The 70A which we all knew closed on the day when Southern Region steam bowed out – 9th July 1967. Today, the whole site which encompassed the various engine sheds at Nine Elms, bares no evidence of railway history and certainly no artefacts of any kind.

Rebuilt Bulleid Pacifics at Nine Elms towards the end! (*above*) Nine Elms own 'WC' No.34017 ILFRACOMBE, looking rather smart, makes its way off shed onto the main line for its next turn of duty in early November 1963. By the end of the month the Pacific would be resident at Eastleigh works undergoing its final 'General' from which it emerged to a new home at Eastleigh shed. This one didn't quite make it to the final day, or even the final year, being withdrawn in October 1966 and later being sold for scrap. (*right*) Twelve months on, in October 1964, one of Bournemouth's 'Merchant Navy' Pacifics No.35027 PORT LINE comes off the coaling road looking half-baked! The flanks appear to have been cleaned whereas the front end has that 'look of the future' which many of the SR engines took on during the final eighteen months or so of steam workings. This engine was another of the late 1966 withdrawals but, after months of storage, it was purchased by a scrap merchant from Barry and the rest is history.

ASHFORD

Ashford shed, like Eastleigh shed, was adjacent to a locomotive works therefore the shed would play host to the engines attending the shops. On 14th April 1958 however this photograph taken outside the south-western corner of the engine shed reveals nothing ex-works, exotic, or even exciting. Centre stage is a filthy Ramsgate based C Class 0-6-0 No.31271 which is flanked by an unidentified 'King Arthur' on the left, and a BR Standard Cl.4 4-6-0, No.75068 from Dover, on the right. What the picture does represent is three generations of motive power; the 'C' from the pre-Grouping period, the 'Arthur' from Southern Railway days, and one of BR's own designs which never had a chance to flower. The engine shed here was one of those erected by the Southern and which was heralded as '.... going to revolutionise shed building.' The prefabricated roof sections, with reinforced concrete walls and supports, became the new labour saving and 'cheaper' components of the future. Or so it seemed. Besides Ashford (which was the last of the concrete buildings), new sheds went up at Dover, Exmouth Junction, Ramsgate. Feltham, built a few years earlier but by the same method, was part L&SW, part Southern and was essentially the first of the concrete sheds. What really happened with the shed started to show itself within a couple of years; leaking joints, corroding concrete and reinforcement bars, and shallow foundations! The Southern had a big problem but with the help of various sealants (lots of it) the shed was made safe – for the time being – but the trouble never really went away and continued to wreak havoc with the building if somewhat arrested by various mastics. The same problems surfaced at the other depots mentioned but none, it seemed, were as acute as Ashford's.

EXMOUTH JUNCTION

As mentioned earlier, BR possessed three of the Adams '0415' class Atlantic or Radial tanks. We've seen one in dire straits on the Eastleigh scrap line so let's go back in time to Wednesday 28th August 1957 and look at one which appears to be in fine fettle. No.30582 basks in the sunshine at Exmouth Junction shed patiently waiting its turn to travel to Axminster shed for further work on the Lyme Regis branch. However, assuming that two engines are working the branch during this busy holiday period, No.30582 would not be going until Saturday (changeover day) for its next week long stint on the branch. Whichever member of the trio returned to Exmouth Junction shed for its washout, a spare was always available to cover failures. Our subject here was built by Robert Stephenson & Co. Ltd. and entered traffic in September 1885 (No.30583 was the oldest by six months and was built by Neilson & Co. Ltd.). No.30582 has a boiler with safety valves in the dome whereas No.30584, the youngest of the trio by three months, had Ramsbottom safety valves on the firebox. 'MN' No.35009 SHAW SAVILL just gets a peek in on the left; this Pacific was a recent acquisition from Salisbury and had just been rebuilt prior to its transfer on 1st April. Note the similarity of shed design when compared with Ashford.

The Exmouth Junction servicing area on 28th August 1957 with two rebuilt Pacifics and an unidentified unrebuilt variant going through the process. Leading the rebuilt pair is 'MN' No.35014 NEDERLAND LINE with No.35017 BELGIAN MARINE beneath the water tank; both were allocated to Nine Elms at this time but carry different levels of cleanliness. Next, it's off to the coaler, then the turntable, ready for home. Exeter was as far west as the Merchant Navy Pacifics were allowed to go. Anywhere beyond was the realm of the 'lightweight' unrebuilt West Country and Battle of Britain Pacifics until the Rebuilt 'WC/BB' were cleared to work beyond St Davids, but then only over the Plymouth road. Throughout the British Railways period, until the Western Region took over in 1963, Exmouth Junction engine shed had the largest concentration of Pacifics on the Southern Region, nearly as many as the whole of the former London Midland & Scottish Railway fleet, and arguably more than any former LNER depot.

GUILDFORD

In late April 1962, a very dirty Q1, No.33005, was photographed at the coaling stage. The steel framed building was some distance away from the engine shed – four-hundred feet or so – and was separated by the road overbridge. The awkwardness of the location at Guildford engine shed prevented the coaling shed being any nearer to the stabling shed although a mechanical plant would probably not have made any difference to the locomotive egress either – although it might have done to the coalmen. This view is looking north with the passenger footbridge from the station, hidden on the right, spanning the sidings beyond.

Anyone travelling by train towards London from a point west of Guildford, would enter a tunnel and, after a short time, would suddenly burst out into daylight and be exposed to a broad vista of railway sheds, yards and a busy passenger station. The engine shed was one of those wonders found mainly on the Southern, the half roundhouse! However, Guildford shed went one better than the pure half-roundhouse design and incorporated a straight shed into the layout served by the turntable. All is revealed in this illustration captured on film from Farnham Road overbridge on the afternoon of Wednesday 25th April 1962. The original half-roundhouse was opened in 1887 and covered thirteen stalls served by a 50ft turntable; that shed was to the right of the turntable. Ten years later a seven road straight shed was added in the space between the existing shed and the main line, its roof nicely showing, from this angle, the north-south axis of the roads beneath. In 1953 British Railways rebuilt the roof using their cheapest, and therefore favourite, method with reclaimed rails clad in corrugated asbestos. The shed appears busy with a 'Mogul' on the turntable, a Q1, No.33015 waiting to use that appliance, and the B4 shed pilot, No.30089, keeping out of the way but ready for action on one of the middle roads. Closing on that fateful day of 7th July 1967, the engine shed was later demolished. Never again would that south-western aspect from Farnham Road look so attractive and animated. On the Down main line, a Drummond '700' class 0-6-0, No.30698 makes its way past the signal box to reverse back onto the Up main and then into the shed precincts for servicing.

3015

A few minutes later, the '700' runs onto the shed passing the unidentified 'Mogul' from the turntable and the Q1 awaiting its turn. Across the main line some superb examples of what is nowadays called 'railway infrastructure' languishes defiantly on an earth-filled, timber-faced platform, challenging progress to come and tear down a hundred years or more of railway servant retreats! I only hope that anyone modelling this section of Guildford station managed to get those ripples correct on the roof of the model of the right-hand building. Although, to be fair, this is a picture of the 1962 period weathered version!

REDHILL

Redhill shed yard as seen from the turntable on 6th March 1961 with a group of Maunsell locomotives all showing their front ends. Two 'V' class 'Schools' are prominent with their wide chimneys – and neglected appearance – Nos.30909 EASTBOURNE and 30914 ST PAULS. Flanking them are two of Redhill's resident U class Moguls, Nos.31616 and 31799, which are in an equally deplorable external condition. The 4-4-0s had been displaced by the expanding Kent Coast electrification and were by now past their prime anyway; No.30914 was just three months away from being condemned whilst No.30909 kept going until February 62'. The shed too appears run-down and neglected but it was 1961 when all things steam was on short notice!

The south end of the shed on 4th December 1962 with a trio of Moguls smartly lined-up but not smartly turned-out. This shed dated from 1853 and was opened by the South Eastern Railway. In 1950 BR performed the usual – BR preferred – roof job but whereas at this, the rear end, they finished off the work with corrugated cladding on the gable, the north end, was given a brick face supported by a concrete lintel.

At the time of Nationalisation, Redhill was one of only two engine sheds in the whole of Surrey (Guildford being the other). Located in the Central Section of the SR., it turned out to be the last depot dealing with steam motive power in that section, and to which it closed on 4th January 1965. However, certain services running into the area still had steam traction and so the depot remained as a servicing point until the following June. In June 1963 when this view was captured, withdrawn engines were filling the tracks at the south end of the shed. U1s Nos.31900 and 31905 were already condemned having succumbed during the previous December, and were nearly ready for hauling away to the scrapyard. On the left N class No.31863 was about to be withdrawn. Note the prefabricated chalet-like structure alongside the rear U1. Were the personnel at Redhill thinking of branching out into the Static Caravan park or Garden Centre business?!

Western Region engines became regular visitors to Redhill shed and one duty would see one of them stabling overnight. On an unrecorded morning in June 1963, 'Manor' No.7806 COCKINGTON MANOR prepares to go off shed in order to head the morning train to Reading South. The 4-6-0 was, at this time, allocated to Oxley shed in Wolverhampton so must have been on loan to Reading shed.

Dated 27th June 1963, this picture shows Rebuilt 'WC' No.34013 OKEHAMPTON visiting the shed at Redhill after working in the day before on a train from Brighton. The north gable of the engine shed, with its flush brick clad screen is just discernible on the left. Note another prefabricated – looks like concrete this one – building stands on the north-west corner of the shed.

2-6-0 No.31790, one of the original U class engines which were rebuilt from the SECR Class K 'River' 2-6-4Ts, comes onto the turntable in the snow at Redhill shed on a crisp, cold and sunny Saturday morning, 2nd January 1965, on what was basically the final full day before the depot's 'official' closure on the following Monday. It was also the last day of steam working on this part of the Central Section of the Southern Region (the final link with steam was the Horsham-Guildford line which was worked by steam with Ivatt tanks until 13th June 1965).